Are We There Yet?

A Zen Journey through Space and Time

Photographs by Peter Cunningham
Excerpts from *Nine-Headed Dragon River* by Peter Matthiessen
Introduction by Bernie Glassman
Afterword by Michel Dobbs

COUNTERPOINT

BERKELEY

Main text is drawn from *Nine-Headed Dragon River*, by Peter Matthiessen, © 1985 by Zen Community of New York. Reprinted by arrangement with Shambhala Publications, Inc., Boston, MA. www.shambhala.com.

Library of Congress Cataloging-in-Publication Data
Matthiessen, Peter.
Are we there yet? : a Zen journey through space and time / by Peter Muryo Matthiessen and Peter Cunningham; introduction by Bernard Glassman.
p. cm.
Selected text from Nine-headed dragon river; photographs published here for the first time.
ISBN 978-1-58243-630-2
1. Matthiessen, Peter. 2. Matthiessen, Peter—Religion. 3. Religious life—Zen Buddhism. 4. Authors, American-20th century—Diaries. 5. Zen Buddhists—United States—Biography. I. Cunningham, Peter, 1947- II. Matthiessen, Peter. Nine-headed dragon river. III. Title.
PS3563.A8584Z475 2010
813'.54—dc22
[B]
2010029481

COUNTERPOINT
1919 Fifth Street
Berkeley, CA 94710
www.counterpointpress.com

Published in cooperation with **Still River Books** www.stillriverbooks.com
Distributed by **Publishers Group West**
Printed in **Canada**
10 9 8 7 6 5 4 3 2 1

TABLE OF CONTENTS

PREFACE

Zen has been called "the religion before religion," which is to say that anyone can practice, including those committed to another faith. And the phrase evokes that natural religion of our early childhood, when heaven and a splendorous earth were one. But soon the child's clear eye is clouded over by ideas and opinions, preconceptions and abstractions. Simple free being becomes encrusted with the burdensome armor of the ego. Not until years later does an instinct come that a vital sense of mystery has been withdrawn. The sun glints through the pines, and the heart is pierced in a moment of beauty and strange pain, like a memory of paradise.

After that day, at the bottom of each breath, there is a hollow place that is filled with longing. We become seekers without knowing that we seek, and at first, we long for something "greater" than ourselves, something apart and far away. It is not a return to childhood, for childhood is not a truly enlightened state. Yet to seek one's own true nature is, as one Zen master has said, "a way to lead you to your long-lost home."

To practice Zen means to realize one's existence moment after moment, rather than letting life unravel in regret of the past and daydreaming of the future. To "rest in the present" is a state of magical simplicity, although attainment of this state is not as simple as it sounds. At the very least, sitting Zen practice, called *zazen*, will bring about a strong sense of well-being, as the clutter of ideas and emotions falls away and body and mind return to natural harmony with all creation. Out of this emptiness can come a true insight into the nature of existence, which is no different from one's Buddha-nature. To travel this path, one need not be a "Zen Buddhist," which is only another idea to be discarded, like "enlightenment" and like "Buddha" and like "God."

Peter Matthiessen

INTRODUCTION

In 1982 I decided to make a pilgrimage to Japan. I had been there countless times before with my teacher, Taizan Hakuyu Maezumi, and even studied there with his teacher, Koryu Osaka. This trip, however, was for the purpose of visiting Zen ancestors, our teachers and their teachers, and the temples and monasteries made famous by the monks who had helped form Japanese Zen.

I asked the man who was to be my first dharma successor, the writer Peter Muryo Matthiessen, to come with me along with the photographer Peter Cunningham. I may have had some inkling back then that the timing was right for that kind of pilgrimage; now, looking back, I see it as a turning point. We were the new generation of Zen practitioners and teachers visiting grandparents, uncles, aunts, and cousins, listening to tales about illustrious forbears, being reminded over and over again about our lineage before, like all new generations, we struck out on our own.

The lineage of our own mispucha, or family, is broad and includes some of Japanese Zen's most dominant modern personalities. Maezumi-roshi, one of a handful of Japanese masters who brought Zen to the West and who founded the Zen Center of Los Angeles, came from a highly regarded, somewhat maverick Dharma family. He received Dharma transmission from his father and root teacher, Baian Hakujun Kuroda, who served as head of the Soto Zen Supreme Court. But he also reached outside the Soto Zen sect to live and study with a Rinzai master by the name of Koryu Osaka, eventually finishing koan study and receiving *inka*, Rinzai's highest teaching empowerment, from him. He also studied koans with Hakuun Yasutani, one of the most illustrious 20th century Zen masters, and received transmission from him as well. While ours is a Soto Zen lineage, it has been deeply influenced by the teachings of these two teachers as absorbed through Maezumi-roshi, and koans continue to be an important study in the Maezumi lineage.

Peter Matthiessen came to us from his own illustrious dharma family. Upon giving Peter priest ordination, Maezumi-roshi had given him the Dharma name of Muryo, which means "boundless." Muryo began his studies with the remarkable Rinzai master Soen Nakagawa, and with his student and successor, Eido Shimano. Our visit to Soen-roshi was one of the highlights of that trip.

On our return from Japan, Muryo was going to lead the first *ango*, or Zen intensive, at the Zen Community of New York, thus becoming my first senior student, and I hoped he would finish his studies with me and become my first Dharma successor. Maezumi-roshi had told me that having a successor was a matter of difficulty and some luck, since it usually involved a lengthy study relationship which could be easily disrupted by the many natural twists and turns that tear people apart. A new project, a new relationship, family tragedy, travel – all these could bring a student-teacher relationship to a pause, and often to an end. As a writer, explorer, naturalist, activist, and spokesman for our planet, Muryo faced many challenges. In fact, during the years of our study together he authored at least one controversial book on Leonard Peltier and the FBI; fought and won an important lawsuit; and continued his writings on the natural world and, of course, his award-winning fiction.

During those years we often had the same conversation again and again, in which Muryo would reproach himself for not dedicating his entire life to the practice and teaching of Zen as our ancestors had done, while I reminded him of Maezumi-roshi's dictum that Zen was all of life, and that his books – nonfiction and fiction – taught a broad audience that often knew nothing of Zen about the interdependence of life. In the end Muryo did indeed finish his studies with me and became my first successor in 1991.

All of this, however, was still ahead of us when, in 1982, we went to visit and pay homage to our ancestors in Japan.

Buddhism traces its roots back to Siddhartha Gautama of the Shakya tribe, who lived in India some 2,500 years ago, and Zen looks back to Bodhidharma's bringing of the teachings from India to China in the early fifth century, signaling the beginning of Chan, which became Zen in Japan. In the lineage charts which Muryo and other successors have drawn, this migration of the teachings from country to country, continent to continent, East to West, is starkly represented in circles and segments of lines in red signifying blood lineage. And indeed, each transition infused and transfused the teachings, heralding the trial and error, changes and adjustments that represented our ancestors' efforts to integrate Zen teachings with their respective cultures and traditions, and make them their own.

The book *Nine-Headed Dragon River* captured the details and flavor of our pilgrimage. Muryo has his own successors now, and Zen is already in its third and fourth generations in America. It is no accident, therefore, that he and I have made subsequent trips together, not to Zen temples but to the Auschwitz-Birkenau concentration camps in Poland and to the Middle East, where I was doing peacemaking work, and I have joined him on safari in Africa, in which I bore witness to his passion and dismay around the harm done to our ecosystems and the large-scale extinction of species of wildlife. As young as Zen is in the West, we are already defining its important intersections with issues governing our very survival, obtaining new life from these old/new teachings and with great patience applying the Buddha's great medicine to our time.

Bernie Glassman
Montague, Massachusetts
New Year's Day 2010

In 1227, at T'ien-t'ung Monastery in southern China, while encouraging Eihei Dogen Zenji to spread the true Dharma in his own land, Japan, his ancestor of North and South, Tendo Nyojo Zenji, presented him with documents of succession, in a silk cover with a design of plum blossoms. These included a document certifying Dogen's place in the circular lineage of the Soto school and a copy of Master Sekito Kisen's "Identity of Relative and Absolute" (*Sandokai*).

"With all sincerity, I give these to you, a foreign monk. I hope you will propagate true Buddhism throughout your country, thereby saving deluded people. Stay clear of kings and ministers, make your home in deep mountains and remote valleys, transmitting the essence of Buddhism forever…"

THE ANCESTORS

THE GREAT ANCESTORS

1. Vipashyin Buddha
2. Shikhin Buddha
3. Vishvabhu Buddha
4. Krakuchchanda Buddha
5. Kanakamuni Buddha
6. Kashyapa Buddha

INDIA

7. Shakyamuni Buddha
8. Mahakashyapa
9. Ananda
10. Shanavasa
11. Upagupta
12. Dhritaka
13. Michaka
14. Vasumitra
15. Buddhanandi
16. Buddhamitra
17. Parshva
18. Punyashas
19. Ashvaghosha
20. Kapimala
21. Nagarjuna
22. Kanadeva
23. Rahulata
24. Sanghanandi
25. Gayashata
26. Kumarata
27. Jayata
28. Vasubandhu
29. Manorhita
30. Haklenayashas
31. Aryasimha
32. Basiasita
33. Punyamitra
34. Prajnatara
35. Bodhidharma

CHINA

36. Daizu Huike
37. Jianzhi Sengcan
38. Dayi Daoxin
39. Daman Hongren
40. Dajian Huineng
41. Qingyuan Xingsi
42. Shitou Xiqian
43. Yaoshan Weiyan
44. Yuntan Tansheng
45. Dongshan Liangjie
46. Yunju Daoying
47. Tongan Daopi
48. Tongan Guanzhi
49. Liangshan Yuanguan
50. Dayang Jingxuan
51. Touzi Yiqing
52. Furong Daokai
53. Danxia Zichun
54. Zhenxie Qingliao
55. Tiantong Zongjue
56. Xuedou Zhijian
57. Tiantong Rujing

JAPAN

58. Eihei Dogen
59. Koun Ejo
60. Tetsu Gikai
61. Keizan Jokin
62. Gasan Joseki
63. Taigen Soshin
64. Baizan Monpon
65. Nyochu Tengin
66. Kisan Shosan
67. Morin Shihan
68. Shoshi Sotai
69. Kenchu Hantetsu
70. Daiju Soko
71. Kinpo Jusen
72. Kajin Sochin
73. Tetsuei Seiton
74. Shukoku Choton
75. Ketsuzan Tetsuei
76. Hoshi Soon
77. Goho Kainon
78. Tenkei Denson
79. Shozan Monko
80. Niken Sekiryo
81. Reitan Roryu
82. Kakujo Tosai
83. Kakuan Ryogu
84. Ryoka Daibai
85. Ungan Guhaku
86. Baian Hakujun
87. Taizan Maezumi

UNITED STATES

88. Bernie Tetsugen Glassman
89. Peter Muryo Matthiessen
90. Michel Engu Dobbs

Zen Journals

Excerpts from *Nine-Headed Dragon River*
Peter Matthiessen 1982

Photographs by
Peter Cunnigham

In 1982, before his formal installation as abbot of the Zen Community of New York's Zen temple, Zenshin-ji, Bernie Tetsugen Glassman-sensei wished to make a pilgrimage to Japan in order to pay formal respects to those teachers, alive and dead, who are associated with his lineage and with his training. In particular, he would visit the ancient places associated with Dogen Zenji, the thirteenth-century Soto Zen master who has emerged in recent years as one of the most exciting minds in the history of thought.

Since I am to be Tetsugen's first head monk, I shall travel with him as his *jisha* or attendant. "After being shuso, you are a senior monk," he says, "and your training enters a new phase. Your knowledge and understanding should be developing into prajna wisdom. Without prajna, you don't really know what you are talking about." Tetsugen feels that, in America, there are too many self-described "Zen teachers" who really don't know what they are talking about, and it is very plain that they embarrass him.

"After I became Maezumi-roshi's first shuso," he says, "I considered myself very lucky to go with him to Japan, but I think it is better that you go beforehand, since being shuso will mean much more to you that way." We would go to the historic Buddhist cities of Kamakura, Nara, and Kyoto; we would visit Maezumi's last living teacher, Osaka Koryu-roshi, who had been one of Tetsugen's teachers, too; and whether or not he chose to see us, we would pay our respects to Nakagawa Soen-roshi at the "Dragon-Swamp Temple," under Mount Fuji.

Hakuyu Taizan Maezumi (1931–1995)

At age fifteen, Maezumi left for Tokyo in order to live and study with the powerful teacher Osaka Koryu-roshi. After four years under Koryu-roshi, Maezumi studied at Komazawa Soto University, in Tokyo. Subsequently he enrolled at Soji-ji, after which he was asked by the Soto administration to go to Los Angeles to assist in the Soto temple founded there in the 1920s. Since his older brother, Kojun Kuroda, would inherit the family temple at Otawara, their father, Baian Hakujun Kuroda approved of the idea, and Maezumi did, too. "I just wanted to go!" he says, and off he went in 1956, at the age of twenty-five. Because the Los Angeles temple had no serious Zen practice, he was happy to learn of "the floating zendo" led by Nyogen Senzaki, with whom he studied until Nyogen's death in 1958.

When Yasutani-roshi came to Los Angeles in 1962, the young monk Maezumi, after asking a few questions, "knew immediately that I should study with him." Yasutani-roshi led sesshin in America almost every year from 1962 to 1969, and his Los Angeles sesshin in 1967 was attended by a young aeronautics engineer named Bernard Glassman. In December 1970, Maezumi completed his studies with Yasutani and received his Dharma seal.

Bernie Tetsugen Glassman

Maezumi-roshi recalls a young Bernie Glassman: "He had a dirty beard! But he also had a flashing light in his eyes, and naiveté in the good sense of the word, open and ready to receive anything he could get. He became an exceptional Zen student because of his devotion to his practice, an ability to hurl himself into whatever he had to do. Very early, he knew how to throw the self away, to become selfless; that's why he could do so well under hard circumstances. He knew what was important and what was unimportant, and he did not waste his time."

"Maezumi-sensei was close to finishing his own koan study, and I had decided to put off my own so that I could begin properly with him when he came back from Japan," says Tetsugen. "But Koryu-roshi's first teisho at that May sesshin was so powerful that I changed my mind. I went to work again on the koan *Mu* as soon as I sat down in the zendo that first day. I really got into it, and by the second day, both Koryu and Maezumi knew that, essentially, I was already there. I wasn't asking any questions, I was just totally immersed. By the third evening, I had passed through it, but Koryu wanted something more from me, wanted me to go deeper, and when I went to dokusan on the fourth morning, I must have been right at the edge of something very powerful. I was still concentrating when I returned to the zendo, and right away I entered a different space, really beautiful, exquisite, very deep.

"All of a sudden, Maezumi-sensei shook me out of that space by really blasting me with '*MU!*' He had seen me come out of dokusan, and knew that I was right on the point of explosion. So after I sat down, he stood right behind me; I don't know how long he stood there, but when he saw that I was really settled in, he yelled '*MU!*' Very loud, right there in the zendo! It broke the logjam; the world just fell apart! So Maezumi took me immediately to the dokusan room and Koryu-roshi confirmed the passing of Mu-ji, and Koryu and I spent about half an hour just hugging and crying – I was overwhelmed. At the next meal – I was head server – tears were pouring down my face as I served Koryu-roshi, and afterwards, when I went out of the zendo – well, there was a tree there, and looking at the tree, I didn't feel I was the tree; it went deeper than that. I felt the wind on me, I felt the birds on me, all separation was completely gone."

Relating this experience, Tetsugen looked slightly uncomfortable, and a bit awed, as if speaking of someone else. Koryu-roshi would later refer to it as one of the most powerful enlightenment experiences he ever witnessed.

"Maezumi-roshi had passed through Mu-ji in his first kensho, after three years of study with Koryu-roshi in Tokyo. He had his second major opening about a year later, while studying at Soji-ji, in Yokohama. I followed a very similar pattern. After that first kensho, I still had doubts about certain things, in particular reincarnation. When I asked Maezumi about it, he would not comment on my questions: he told me to reread the letters on the subject in *The Three Pillars of Zen*, then work on the question myself. And one day when I was reading one of these letters in a car going to work – I was in a car pool, and my office was about an hour from the Zen Center – and a powerful opening occurred right in the car, much more powerful than the first. One phrase triggered it, and all my questions were resolved. I couldn't stop laughing or crying, both at once, and the people in the car were very upset and concerned, they didn't have any idea what was happening, and I kept telling them there was nothing to worry about!" Tetsugen laughed. "Luckily I was an executive and had my own office, but I just couldn't stop laughing and crying, and finally I had to go home.

"That opening brought with it a tremendous feeling about the suffering in the world; it was a much more compassionate opening than the first. I saw the importance of spreading the Dharma, the necessity to develop a Dharma training in America that would help many people. Until then, I had believed in strong zazen, in 'forcing' people, using the kyosaku. That method encourages kensho, but the effects are not so deep and lasting, and anyway, it doesn't work for everybody. I wanted to work with greater numbers because I saw the 'crying out' of all of us, even those who feel they are not crying out. And that second opening had nothing to do with the zendo atmosphere, or working on a koan. The major opening can occur anywhere; we never know when it's going to happen.

"Personally, I don't stress openings, or talk about them, because I don't want people to get caught up in that. Yet I think kensho is essential – it has to happen. And so long as the practice is constant and steady, so long as the student continues to practice without being intent on achieving some 'special' state, something that he or she has heard about, it will. When the idea of gain falls away, people open up. That's why a teacher is important – to keep the student from getting caught up in some incomplete idea of what it's all about, and forcing his zazen in that direction."

Peter Muryo Matthiessen

During morning service, I chanted with such intensity that I "lost" myself, obliterated my self – a function of the ten-line Kannon Sutra, dedicated to the bodhisattva Avalokiteshvara, which is chanted hard, over and over, thirty-three times, with wood gong and bells, in mounting volume and intensity. At the end, the chanters give one mighty shout of '*MU!*'– which symbolizes the Absolute, universality – this followed instantly by a great hush of sudden, ringing silence, as if the universe had stopped to listen. But on this morning, in the near darkness – the altar candle was the only light in the long room – this immense hush swelled and swelled and kept on swelling, as if this "I" were opening out into infinity, in eternal amplification of my Buddha-being. There was no hallucination, only awe. "I" had vanished and also "I" was everywhere.

Then I let my breath go, gave myself up to immersion in all things, to a joyous belonging so overwhelming that tears of relief poured from my eyes. For the first time since unremembered childhood, I was not alone, there was no separate "I." Wounds, anger, ragged edges, hollow places were all gone; all had been healed; my heart was the heart of all creation. Nothing was needed, nothing missing; all was already, always, and forever present and forever known.

In this very breath that we take now lies the secret that all great teachers try to tell us, what one lama refers to as "the precision and openness and intelligence of the present." The purpose of meditation practice is not enlightenment; it is to pay attention even at unextraordinary times, to be of the present, nothing-but-the-present, to bear this mindfulness of now into each event of ordinary life. To be anywhere else is "to paint eyeballs on chaos." When I watch blue sheep, I must watch blue sheep, not be thinking about sex, danger, or the present, for this present – even while I think of it is gone.

(from *Snow Leopard/Himalayan Journal*)

Koryu-roshi (1901–1987)

Maezumi-roshi wished to visit his last living teacher, Osaka Koryu-roshi, who lives at Hannya [Prajna] Dojo, a Zen training center constructed a half century ago in what is now Inogashira Park, in northern Tokyo. The modest building, like a hermitage, lies half hidden in dark woods that overlook a narrow, leafy pond. At the age of eighty, Koryu-roshi is still noted for his powerful teisho and dramatic dokusan, and continues to maintain stem discipline with his students. He is nearly blind from a deteriorating eye condition apparently caused by exposure to the first atomic blast at Hiroshima, which burned off his hair before he could jump into a shelter.

"When koans were made, there was the attempt to put all of Buddhism into a single phrase," Koryu-roshi has said. "What is the Buddha? Why did the Patriarch come from the West? Zen seeks to speak the entirety of the Buddha's teaching in a single phrase. But the odor of 'Buddhism' remains. Hakuin simply put out one hand and said, 'Hear this!' This is truly put directly to us, completely apart from all the trappings of 'Buddhism.' To hear the sound of one hand, our fundamental nature must clearly come forth. Without using the word 'Buddha,' without using the word 'Zen,' we throw ourselves directly into the recesses of the mind."

Happily the old teacher relates how his excellent student, Taizan Maezumi, cataloged the dojo library of 60,000 volumes. The soft voice falls and rises like the spring wind that murmurs all around the old wood house as the roshi's wife offers a light repast of sashimi – raw sea bass, tuna, mackerel, crayfish, fish roe, and squid, served with soy sauce, green mustard, radish, and raw ginger – set about with pickled cauliflower and carrot, mustard tofu, nori, and early strawberries.

"The seed of Zen was sown in India, its flower blossomed in China, and in Japan it bore fruit," Koryu-roshi has said. "In Japan we savor Zen through an extraordinarily wide range of things. In this room flowers have been arranged, bringing nature in, and if we open the screens here, a garden will lie before us. Nature is constantly being brought in.... I think that in putting a vast world into something small, there is the 'wondrous flavor' of Zen."

(Koryu-roshi died on July 27, 1987.)

Unbroken Practice

This life of one day is a life to rejoice in.
Because of this, even though you live for just one day,
if you can be awakened to the truth,
that one day is vastly superior to an eternal life.
If this one day in the lifetime of a hundred years is lost,
will you ever get your hands on it again?

Eihei Dogen

Fuji-san

The road passed a closed amusement park with soiled pastel walls banged by the breeze. A chemical-colored polar bear was king of a plastic ice floe in the middle of a large plastic lagoon. Higher still, in the "Fuji Safari Park," a few chilled golfers swatted balls across last winter's novice ski slope. The road came to an end well below the snows at a "Wildlife Protection Area," a small forest without the smallest sign of life. In vain did I scan the silent woods for ashy minivets and red-flanked bluetails, green woodpeckers and copper pheasants, while Tetsugen, who discourses as freely as the uguisu sings, kept up an animated conversation. Chido-sensei walked ahead of us, hands tucked up behind his back, muttering a little, and seeing the snow cone through the trees beyond him, I was reminded of a story told by Soen-roshi, to show how words get in the way of the natural expression of the thing itself.

One day a young monk at Ryutaku-ji had a kensho, and his teacher, seeking to deepen this experience, led him on a long walk up Mount Fuji. Although the monk had seen the great snow mountain many times before, he truly perceived it now for the first time (like the monk who truly perceived that the sun was round), and all the way up, he kept exclaiming over the harmony and colors of the wildflowers, the flight of birds, the morning light in the fresh evergreens, the sacred white mountain rising in mighty silence to the sky. "Look, Roshi, this pine cone! See how it is made? That stone, it's so … so stone! Isn't it wonderful? Do you hear the nightingale? It is a miracle! Oh! Fuji-san!"

Muttering a little, the old master hobbled onward, until finally his student noticed his long silence and cried out, "Isn't it so? Aren't these mountains, rivers, and great earth miraculous? Isn't it beautiful?" The old man turned on him. "Yes-s-s," he said forcefully. "But what a pity to say so!"

The Kuroda-Maezumi Family

Tetsugen-sensei, who had first met Baian Hakujun in 1970, was "impressed by his emphasis on *aigo*, loving words. It was very rare for him to be harsh with anyone. He always had guests at his temple, and his staff and family were always serving. Privacy was never an issue, since they had none; theirs was a life of giving and serving. He never accumulated money, but spent it on the members, guests, and the temple. Money was an energy source that flowed. This kind of lived patience and lived caring is very rare. His teaching was his life, lived in everyday situations, the kind of undramatic teaching that seeps into the blood and marrow of a student and transforms him. Of course such transformation takes many years, but it is the transmission of the true Dharma."

As the second son, Maezumi-roshi took his mother's family name – a traditional custom that keeps an old family from dying out – but he still regards this temple as his home. With Kuroda-roshi's family, and Baian Hakujun's sprightly widow, known as Obachan (Grandmother), we relaxed at a fine homecoming supper, toasting the coming together at Koshin-ji with copious amounts of sake. Then we drank more in celebration of the coming of Buddhism to America, Europe, and Israel, which would one day be recognized as a great historical event.

It's a family regimen which the Kuroda brothers have made famous in Zen circles, Maezumi celebrated with sake and whiskey until after midnight, then rose the next morning before dawn. Peevish, he expressed annoyance that his American students had not risen in time to do zazen before morning service. When I murmured that our sluggishness might be accounted for by all that drink, Maezumi snapped, "Sake is one thing and zazen is another! They have nothing to do with each other!"

Kuroda-roshi led an elaborate service in which we moved from altar to altar, hall to hall. Afterward we went outside and climbed the hillside to the grave of Baian Hakujun, on a rise overlooking the old town. Obachan, out early to cut daffodils, hobbled stolidly up the steep hill behind us, and Maezumi-roshi, already recovered, called out happily, "Ho, Obachan!" in affirmation of his mother's existence.

At the grave, we offered water, incense, flowers. The north wind of recent days had died, and the clear skies were thickening with a change of weather. All the way up to the evergreen forest on the ridge, soft, shifting light filled the cherry blossom clouds that covered the hillside. The earth was sprinkled with the blue of violets, and the mist of pale pink cherry blossoms was quickened here and there by blood-red and bone-white camellias. Noisy flocks of bulbuls, with a few bold jays, crossed the high trees, and the wild pigeons mourned their ancestors back in the wood.

The Suzuki Family

Hoichi Suzuki-sensei is the son of Shunryu Suzuki-roshi, former abbot of Rinso-in at Yaizu, on the southern coast, who later founded the Zen Center in San Francisco. In 1971, at Tassajara, the Center's retreat deep in the Coast Range, I worked briefly as an assistant to the carpenter monk who was putting a new roof on the cottage of Suzuki-roshi. Although he was dying, the roshi evinced the keenest interest in our progress, and this interest provided a wonderful opportunity to observe the comings and goings of this gentle teacher, who still offered teisho in the evening. Suzuki-roshi was already frail, and one day his jisha, cleaning his room, set down his teacup a little too hard in her rush to assist him at the doorway. "Take care of my cup!" he warned her mildly. And when she protested that her only wish was to take care of her teacher, the roshi said, "When you take care of my cup, you are taking care of me."

The carpenter monk was engaged to marry this young woman, who was rich. Since he himself had always been penniless, the prospect of money worried him; he told me he had expressed this worry to Suzuki-roshi. "Rich or poor, it does not matter," the roshi told him. "It only matters if you cling to being rich." He smiled in warning. "Or poor." The monk nodded uncertainly, saying he understood. "Since you understand," the roshi said, "then you may as well be rich."

"My father wished to bring zazen way to other countries," says Suzuki-sensei, an appealing man with a sad face and a quick laugh who had welcomed us the previous evening to Rinso-in, near the fishing village of Yaizu. The night wind of April off the North Pacific was dank and cold, and we were grateful for Hoichi-san's green tea, sweet cakes, and Napoleon brandy. Expressing regret that he could not speak English as well as his father, he defeated Tetsugen-sensei in a game of go. "First my father went to China, but under that government, the people are only coming back very slowly to Buddhism, and it does not work there. So the Soto headquarters in Tokyo suggests San Francisco, and my father is willing. He studied some English in middle school, and maybe he wanted to use it. So in San Francisco he put up just a little card outside. It said, 'Everybody welcome, come and sit zazen.' That was, I think, in 1962. And it built up slowly, slowly, in a natural way."

Together with Maezumi-roshi, who preceded him by a few years in America, Suzuki-roshi is revered as the founder of Soto Zen practice in the United States, and his gentle teisho, assembled in *Zen Mind, Beginner's Mind,* are widely read by Zen students in the West. In December 1971, a few months after my visit to Tassajara, this wonderful teacher died of cancer. Eido-roshi, who had gone to California to attend him not long before his death, was extremely impressed. He told his students upon his return to New York City, "Shunryu Suzuki was a true-ue-e ro-shi!"

Shunryu Suzuki's grave lies under evergreens up the small stream that comes down the forested ravine behind Rinso-in, a pretty temple built in the fifteenth century. In April the shady margins of the stream are lighted by large blue-and-yellow orchids. We offer incense in spring morning light as swallow-tailed butterflies come and go in red-striped arabesques, mindlessly offering the bold red dots on the undersides of their black wings.

THERE IS NO ONE ON THIS ROAD BUT ME THIS AUTUMN EVENING.

BASHO

Eihei-ji

To reach Eihei-ji, which remains today the best-known Zen monastery in the world, one travels by small electric train, sixteen kilometers inland from Fukui, ascending the valley of the Nine-Headed Dragon River to the steep village that has accumulated over the centuries at Eihei-ji's gates. Here a wood plaque inscribed with Chinese characters reads, "Only those concerned with life and death need enter here." Rebuilt after a fire in the fifteenth century, Eihei-ji today is composed of some seventy buildings, yet this huge place seems overwhelmed by the looming hoary cedars on the mountainside, the rush of water.

At the guest hall we are given formal tea by Hirano-sensei, guest master at Eihei-ji, a cool, urbane, and handsome priest. Subsequently two apprentice monks, or *unsui* (from an old Chinese verse, "to drift like clouds and flow like water"), lead us to the baths, then bring a simple supper to our room.

There is an old mountain bell that each new monk must sound upon his arrival at Eihei-ji. "What do you want here!" the older monks bellow at him, in the first test of his resolve. From that day forward, the unsui run barefoot from duty to duty and from job to job. "A monk is like the clouds and has no fixed abode; like flowing water he has nothing to depend on." In black work denims, white cloths wrapped around their naked heads, squads of grim youths attack ceaseless cleaning of the stairs and corridors, stopping short to bow almost to the waist to the lowliest priest, then resuming their arduous and redundant work, performed barefoot even in the winter.

In the darkness, deep in the April mountains, it is very cold. A bell awakens the unsui, and there comes a hushed stir as the monks clamber about, folding their bed rolls into the lockers on the tatami platforms. Within ten minutes they are dressed and seated in zazen, and soon the monitor is making his rounds with the narrow-bladed stick that represents Manjusri's delusion-cutting sword. The old timbers echo the monotonous whack-whack on each pair of shoulders. The somber priest does not spare the gaijin – *whack!* – the pain rings in my ears. Then he is gone and each black-robed figure sits alone in the cold gloom of the old brown hall with what Maezumi-roshi calls "the Real One inside ourselves."

Later, Tetsugen says, "For Dogen, the Zen of our everyday life, moment after moment, is truly the way of enlightenment. His great contribution – and his own life was an example – was the perception that daily practice and enlightenment are one. That's why his system here at Eihei-ji became so ritualized – so that his whole life and being could become a model for what our life should be. Part of Dogen's plan in ritualizing Eihei-ji was the emphasis he put on everyday life, on work and personal conduct, as opposed to koan study, teisho, and dokusan.

"The one way to be truly universal is to be very particular, moment by moment, detail by detail. If you are merely 'universal,' you lose the feel of life; you become abstract, facile. But if the emphasis on everyday detail is too rigid, our existence loses the religious power of the universal. To walk with one foot in each world – that was Dogen's way, and Dogen's life. In a single sentence, he talked from both points of view, the absolute and the relative, the universal and the particular. He was not only living in both, he was switching so fast between the two that he was in neither! He was entirely free! And this is wonderful, just as it should be!"

At the end of zazen, while still seated, we put on the toga-like Buddha's robe, or *kesa*, and also white bessu on our bare feet, after which we climb the steps to the main service hall. Waiting for the service to begin, we stand outside on a platform overlooking the monastery below. Dawn is coming, and still it is very cold. The gray-tiled roofs are dim in the night's shadow, but the climbing sky high overhead, behind evergreen turrets on the ravine walls, is turning pale, and already a solitary bird sings in the forest. Not far from here, on a rock outcrop above the lower buildings, Dogen Kigen is said to have performed outdoor zazen.

In the great hall we take our place in long rows of gold-robed priests and black-robed monks. The chanting and invocations of the morning service last almost two hours, most of it kneeling, sitting on our heels. For one unbroken stretch of nearly an hour we maintain this position which Japanese use all their lives but which for most Westerners becomes painful rather quickly.

American students never last long at Eihei-ji, which is the most rigorous and austere of all Soto monasteries and has small tolerance for lack of fortitude; for years, this place refused to accept American students, who were not worth the bother of having to deal with their complaints.

The long service is choreographed against the golden altar, the cascades of small golden bells, the scarlet carpeting on the tatami mats. The pageantry, the bells, the pound of voices to ancient drums is stirring, and we, too, chant those parts of the service that, in our training, we have memorized in Japanese: the Heart Sutra; the *Sandokai* (" The Identity of Relative and Absolute"), the *Names of the Patriarchs*, and the *Daihishin Dharani*. Toward the end, an old priest beckons us, and I follow Tetsugen to the main altar, where we make our bows and offer incense.

Even in bright morning sun, the power of the place is not dispelled. Most monasteries are located in the mouths of valleys, but here, the old buildings sit in a compact mass in the deep V made by the mountainsides, high up in the dark ravine of the Nine-Headed Dragon River. Because its buildings are necessarily close together, the old monastery has great force, for as Dogen teaches us, Eihei-ji itself is doing zazen, hurling its power down the canyon and out into the world on every toll of the old mountain bell.

From Kanazawa northeastward to the Noto Peninsula, the local train crosses a plain of rice fields among humble mountains. The paddies in wet browns and greens are set off by lone white egrets, like sentinels. Spring comes late to this northern land, and the rice is in several stages of seasonal cycle: a cracked winter earth of withered stalks is side by side with dark rectangles of froggy water and patches of intense fresh green.

Today I am a Soto monk, not yet white-haired or sparse of tooth but older and more scarred than my fresh-faced teacher. Isshin-Mugaku-Muryo stares out the window. I have never cared much for Dharma names, which strike me as "extra" in the context of American Zen. Yet they serve as a reminder (I suppose) not to cling to the badge of identity in my given name – the illusion of separation, which is ego – but to aspire as best I can to One Mind, Dream Awakening, Without Boundaries. Sometimes in zazen on my black cushion I approach these states.

The train follows around the shore through a small series of fishing towns stuck to the coast between the hills and sea. Small rice fields abut the sea walls, even the beaches, and one paddy, scarcely twenty feet across, is pinched between the railroad tracks and a row of pines along the cliff, above blue water.

Waves recede.

Not even the wind ties up a small abandoned boat.

The moon is a clear mark of midnight.

Once again, the ephemeral and the universal: Dogen called this poem "On the Treasury of the True Dharma Eye" as if to point out that these simple lines conveyed the whole import of his mighty work.

Small flocks of sandpipers on their way to Kamchatka and the Siberian tundra cross back and forth over the gleaming fields, and a Japanese pheasant flutters across a ditch, cocks its head in the spring sun, then sneaks into the thin margin of weeds. A man planting his new field casts grain from side to side as he wades in yellow boots through the shallow water, and the grains wrinkle the bland surface like quick puffs of wind, startling Siberian buntings that flit away along the grassy strips between the paddies. But there is no wind, and when he has gone, the water reflects a big white cloud that passes over between sea and mountain.

So-in Soji-ji

The train stops at Anamizu on the bay, from where a small bus huffs uphill over the dry wooded ridge of the Noto Peninsula and wheezes down again on noisy air brakes to the valley of the Haka River. Here at the base of a small mountain stands the monastery that Keizan founded in 1321. Since then the village of Monzen has grown up around it, while the Haka delta was transformed into broad rice fields. The old monastery, an airy and open space along a long court at the base of the hill, was rebuilt after the most recent fire in the late 1800s. It has been called So-in Soji-ji, or "Old Soji-ji" since 1907, when Soji-ji was officially moved to its present location in Yokohama, south of Tokyo, as one of the two head temples of the Soto sect.

At So-in Soji-ji the abbot was away, but his assistant and the ten-odd monks who take care of the old monastery were friendly and hospitable, offering green tea and nori crackers in a guest chamber that overlooked an enclosed garden of ilex and small pines. At Eihei-ji there had been no contact with any unsui except those who served us, but here we slurped thin Japanese noodles in exuberant Japanese style at the monks' table and took the morning meal with them after zazen and the sutra-chanting service the next day.

That afternoon we walked down the valley of the Haka to the sea. Gulls, terns, herons, and an osprey had convened around the calm waters of an estuary pool behind the beach, and a pretty fishing village sat perched at the river's mouth, but the beach was disfigured by the wrack of plastic and industrial flotsam left stranded on the sand after each tide. The eager materialism of a small and crowded country has deprived the Haka delta of its "life integrity" as an ocean shore.

Soji-ji

Since 1907, when it moved from the remote Noto Peninsula to Yokohama, Soji-ji has replaced Eihei-ji as the largest temple of the Soto sect. The new monastery's location in a pleasant, open, park-like area of a big city denies it the power of that ancient place on the Nine-Headed Dragon River, in the mountains; the atmosphere is less severe, and all but novice monks may greet and smile. But the 200-yard corridor that links the monastery to the entrance building is cleaned and shined three times a day by the squads of unsui, who, as at Eihei-ji, must lock into deep bows each time a superior sweeps past.

Before daylight, roused by an old and crippled monk, we were led to the guest zendo across the corridor from the monks' hall. Dawn zazen was followed by morning service in the hondo, where Tetsugen and I, on our knees in the gold-and-black-robed rows, could study the intricate precision of the ritual. Swift monks ran backward from the altar, snatching up sutra books in stacks for presentation to the priests, who deftly flared the saffron pages in symbolic readings of the sacred texts.

Later, the monks and preceptors had gathered for Dharma combat. Whoever wished to benefit from the zenji's Dharma might now rush forward between ranks of priests to face the zenji in his staff and hood, high on the altar. Each cried out his question, and the zenji answered in a calm and measured voice, then banged his stave as the aspirant ran backward from the altar, crying out shrilly once again in gratitude.

At this altar, just five years ago, Tetsugen-sensei had officiated at the morning service, having been installed as temporary abbot of Soji-ji the night before. When repeated at Eihei-ji, this zuise ceremony completed his priestly training in the Soto school.

Buddha-Nature

This the very impermanence of grass and tree, thicket and forest, is the Buddha-nature. The very impermanence of men and things, body and mind, is the Buddha-nature. Nations and lands, mountains and rivers are impermanent because they are the Buddha-nature. Supreme and complete enlightenment, because it is the Buddha-nature, is impermanent....

Our present moment-to-moment activity is the opening of a gate.... Completely utilizing life, we cannot be held back by life. Completely utilizing death, we cannot be bothered by death. Do not cherish life. Do not blindly dread death. They are where the Buddha-nature is.

For infinite kalpas in the past, foolish people in great numbers have regarded man's spiritual consciousness as Buddha-nature, or as man's original state of suchness – how laughably absurd!... Buddha-nature is a fence, a wall, a tile, a pebble.

Eihei Dogen

History

Thirteen centuries ago the Mahayana teachings arrived in the backward islands known to the Chinese as "the Land of Wa." Early Buddhism in Japan was not yet "Zen," although Zen traces may have been apparent: Japanese visitors to China, staying close to the cities and old monastic centers, had little exposure to the new "Zen" school which was developing in China's southern mountains.

By the middle of the sixth century, the first sutra books and Buddhist relics had turned up in Japan. Unlike India, where the teachings of Shakyamuni had to compete with Hinduism and Vedanta – and unlike China with its Taoism and Confucian law – Japan had no philosophical religion or literate priesthood, no body of teachings, or a written language. The early peoples who had arrived over long ages from the mainland coasts lived in shifting settlements along the rivers and practiced an indigenous form of sun and nature worship (later called Shinto, "the Way of the Gods"). Therefore these first holy objects, accompanied by a written language, made a great stir in the rude assemblies that history books refer to as the imperial courts.

Soon there were more than forty Buddhist temples in this region, complete with relics, priestly vestments, and colorful ceremonies to attract the people. Most of these ceremonies, as in Shinto, were devoted to curing, summoning rain for crops, and other practical considerations. Enthusiasm in imperial court circles for the new culture from "the Land of T'ang" was evident in the foolhardy adoption of the complicated Chinese ideographs for the relatively simple Japanese language, and a somewhat less disastrous decision to replicate a Chinese city in Japan. Until now there had been no capital town in the islands. The new "Central City" of Nara, some forty miles inland from the present Osaka, was eventually laid out in A.D. 710, and remains a Buddhist shrine twelve centuries later.

It was possibly rampant corruption that encouraged the decision, in 793, to remove the court to Kyoto, which was to become one of the largest cities in the world, with a population that may well have approached a half-million people, but as at Nara, there was little about it that could be called Japanese. Every aspect of its culture, from its architecture to its etiquette, was a painstaking imitation of T'ang dynasty culture in China.

In 788, an inspired eighteen-year-old monk named Saicho withdrew from Nara to the high forests on Mount Hiei west of Kyoto to escape the rigid structures and corruption of the priesthood and to renew Shakyamuni's emphasis on meditation. Saicho established a twelve-year course in religious studies that would make Mount Hiei the greatest school of religion in the nation, and it was in his Tendai temple, known today as Enryaku-ji, that most of the later schools of Buddhism would have their start. But Japanese Buddhism remained a pale, priest-ridden imitation of the Chinese schools, since the great teaching lineages that ensured the continuity of the true Dharma had not yet made their way across the China Sea.

Toward the end of the twelfth century, a Tendai priest called Eisai received Dharma transmission in the Oryu branch of Rinzai Zen. Eisai deplored what had become of the old Buddhism on Mount Hiei. His proposed reforms won the approval of the shogun, who sponsored the construction of Kennin Temple, in Kyoto. Kennin-ji deferred to the older sects by including Tendai and Shingon subtemples, but Master Eisai, nonetheless, might be called the first Zen teacher in Japan.

In Zen tradition, there is a saying, "Only be ready, and the teacher will appear." Apparently the Land of Wa was ready, for the first true teachers and strong teaching lineages were emerging, even as Zen in China was on the wane.

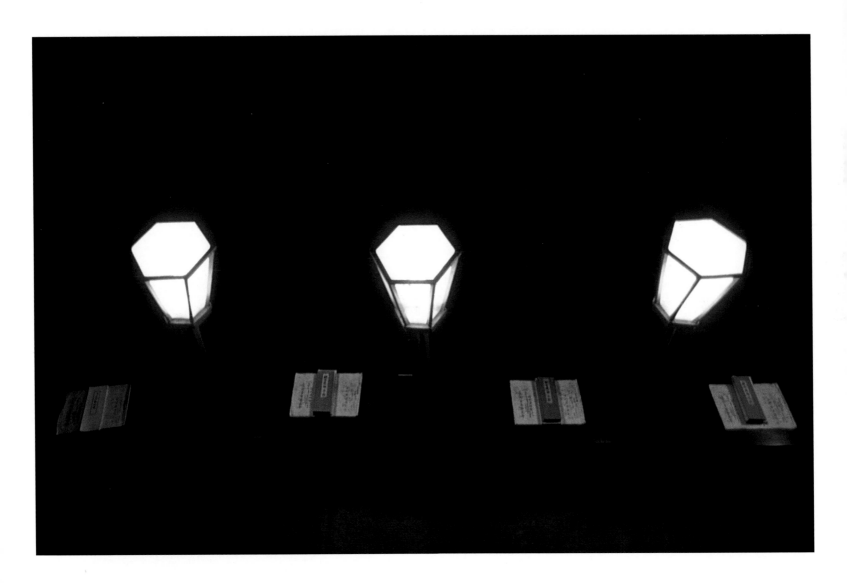

Eihei Dogen Zenji (1200–1253)

In the last decades of the twelfth century, the Heian aristocracy preoccupied itself with art and poetry in the Chinese style, infused by *mujo*, a rarefied, romantic sense of life's impermanence, often symbolized in the fall of cherry blossoms in spring. On the second day of the thirteenth century a child was born in Kyoto who would have a precocious experience of life's impermanence, since he seems to have been illegitimate and would soon be orphaned. "At his mother's funeral, observing the smoke of incense, he intimately realized the impermanence of the world of sentient beings, and profoundly developed the great aspiration to seek the Dharma."

For the rest of his life, Dogen was concerned with the awakening of the enlightened state through penetration of the true nature of reality, and the consequent freedom from the bondage of life and death, as in his own image – a fish escaping from the net. "At each moment," he would write, "do not rely upon tomorrow. Think of this day and this hour only, and of being faithful to the Way, for the next moment is uncertain and unknown."

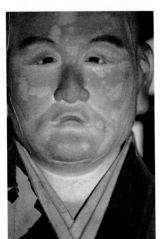

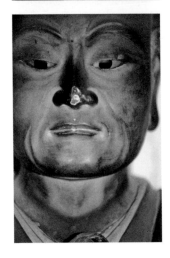

In 1213 Dogen trudged up Mount Hiei to Enryaku-ji. Here the Tendai abbot Koen gave him the precepts in a small temple on a wooded ledge under the north peak, on a steep hillside of giant cedars. That temple burned to the ground in 1942.

We were eager to experience the place where Monk Dogen received ordination; an obliging young priest led us downhill on the silent forest paths to the remains of the old temple, which is marked by an open-air altar scattered with needles from the tall and silent trees. Probably the oldest conifers on this mountainside were already living when that thirteen-year-old boy, pate fresh and shining as an apple seed, received his monk's robe and monk's bowl from Koen, with the blue cloud mirror of Lake Biwa shining below.

In Dogen's time, Enryaku-ji concerned itself with rituals and rich ceremonies that attracted the costumed aristocracy of Kyoto, paying small attention to the practice of the Buddha's teachings. It made much of Shakyamuni's realization that "all sentient beings have the Buddha-nature," since this seemed to eliminate the need for arduous training. Dogen (who would teach that Shakyamuni meant "All beings are the Buddha-nature") demanded of his mentors why, in that case, the Buddhist Patriarchs had struggled so hard to attain this enlightened condition. Already he knew that priestly finery, ritual incense burning, sacrament and ceremony, sutra copying and even chanting – the mere veneration of the Buddha's words – all missed the point, that the structured hierarchies of Mount Hiei had lost the bold spirit of the quest for profound awakening.

In the Land of Sung, as in the Land of Wa, the Buddhist priesthood was enmeshed in politics, finance, and the imperial court. Young Dogen, already contemptuous of the immature Buddhism in Japan, was dismayed by its decrepitude in China; he soon despaired of finding a true teacher of the uncompromising kind he had read about in the ancient Chinese chronicles.

Indeed, the closest Dogen came to the pure spirit of Zen was an encounter with an old monastery cook in the first days after his arrival. This monk, who had visited his ship to buy Japanese mushrooms, declined Dogen's invitation to stay and converse, since he had to get back to his monastery to supervise the next day's meals. When Dogen protested, saying that other cooks would surely take care of things, the old man said mildly that his job as *tenzo*, or head cook, was "my training during my old age. How can I leave this duty to others?" Incredulous, Dogen exclaimed, "Venerable sir! Why don't you do zazen, or study the koan of ancient masters? What is the use of working so hard as tenzo monk?" At this the cook laughed, remarking that the young Japanese appeared ignorant of the meaning of true training, much less Buddhism.

In the cook's reproof lay two important teachings which were later much emphasized by Dogen, that work for its own sake was fundamental in Zen practice, and that the state of enlightenment was manifest in even the most ordinary acts of everyday life.

From 1223 to 1225, Dogen visited a number of the leading monasteries of southern China, after which, having failed to find a teacher, he decided to return home to Japan. But at T'ien-t'ung, the Rinzai abbot had been replaced by a teacher of the Soto sect named Ju-ching (Tendo Nyojo), who until this time had led the life of a poor wandering monk, far from the influences of the government and court. More interesting still, so far as Dogen was concerned, was Ju-ching's repudiation of priestly occupations and his insistence on strict training based on shikantaza. "No more need," said Ju-ching, "to burn incense, make prostrations, invoke buddhas, perform repentance ceremonies, or read scriptures – just sit and liberate mind and body."

"I met Master Ju-ching face-to-face!" Dogen wrote later, extremely moved by his first meeting with a severe master who shunned fame, fine robes, and monetary privilege, and who, in his enlightened old age, did zazen until late each night, beginning again early each morning, vowing "to wear out a diamond seat." Dogen, who had all but abandoned hope of finding an inspired teacher, immediately recognized this one, in whom "living and understanding correspond to each other."

Dogen spent three years at T'ien-t'ung, entering wholeheartedly into rigorous zazen practice. One day during meditation, Ju-ching shouted at a sleeping monk, "When you study under a master, you must drop body and mind! What's the use of single-minded intense sleeping?" For Dogen, seated right beside this monk, the shouted words "drop body and mind!" precipitated a profound kensho. He made his way to the abbot's quarters and burned incense in awe and gratitude, and after a brief exchange, Ju-ching confirmed that his young Japanese disciple had indeed "dropped body and mind." The unrelenting Dogen said, "It might have been a temporary delusion; please do not give me the seal of approval indiscriminately!" Apparently this was his way of pleading that his teacher drive him deeper, which he did, and eventually Dogen left after receiving face-to-face Dharma transmission: "The Great Matter of my life was thus resolved." He had now perceived that "Buddha-nature is not some kind of changeless entity, but is none other than the eternally rising and perishing reality of the world" – the wonderful precision of this present moment, moment after moment – now! – just as the old cook had tried to teach him.

"I have returned to my native country with empty hands. There is not even a hair of Buddhism in me. Now I pass the time naturally; the sun rises in the east every morning, and every night the moon sets in the west. When the clouds clear, the outline of the mountains appears, and as the rain passes away, the surrounding mountains bend down. What is it, after all?"

In effect Dogen had freed himself of all ideas and preconceptions about Buddhism, about enlightenment, about the true nature of reality, all of which had "dropped away with body and mind." There was simply the fact of his vertical nose and horizontal eyes, of the sun and moon rising and falling, moment by moment, day by day. With the opening of his true Dharma eye, he perceived the extraordinary within the ordinary, and realized with all buddhas and patriarchs that everything, everywhere, in every moment is "nothing special," as is said in Zen, being complete and perfect just-as-it-is.

In his efforts to adapt Dogen's "Chinese" teachings to the Japanese people, Keizan Jokin felt obliged to give these teachings a name. Like Ju-ching, Dogen had put much more emphasis on the way of everyday enlightenment than on the Zen sect and its various schools, but his successors, attempting to claim him by setting his teachings apart, established a Japanese Soto school, naming Dogen and Keizan its cofounders. Dogen would surely have abominated the proselytizing of his teachings, not to speak of the defiling of the Dharma in the esoteric prayers and tantric incantations adapted from Shingon by his followers to broaden Soto's appeal. Yet but for Keizan and other missionaries, Japanese Soto and Dogen's teachings might never have endured to the present day.

Kyoto

Kennin-ji in Dogen's days was located in a wooded swamp along the Kamo River, in Kyoto. Since then the Kamo has been rechanneled and the swampland drained, and the modern city has grown up around it, replacing the miasmal climate of the swamp with that of the Gion red-light district.

According to an American monk, Thomas Kirchner, Shaku Yuho, Kennin-ji is the most active Rinzai training center in Kyoto, and one of the few monasteries left in Japan that maintains a strict zazen schedule. Seven days a week, as in the old days, thirtyone monks arise at 4:00 A.M. for zazen, then go out into the city with their "begging bowls." In the afternoon the monks perform their monastery duties, followed by zazen until near midnight. They are also expected to chant sutras every day, at two in the afternoon and at two in the morning.

On the day of our visit, a special ceremony was in progress. Outside the entrance to the main service hall was a hallucinatory array of hundreds of small Japanese shoes, set out in intricate patterns to help the wearer locate the right pair upon emerging. Within, small, bright-robed, decorous figures moved ceremonially across a sun-filled hall.

The event in progress was an annual commemoration of the importation of green tea by Master Eisai, who had used it as a stimulant for his monks during zazen. Under the stern eye of elder roshis, four leading tea masters, each with eight disciples, were being served tea in high ceremonial fashion by the priests and monks, after which formal tea would be prepared for two hundred or more Japanese ladies in ornate combs and many-colored silks. Tiny feet in their white tabi peeped like mice from beneath their silks as the happy ladies, opening bright fans, sailed across the fresh-smelling greenish straw of new tatami.

In the stone garden, a turtle dove's wings were the bronze color of wild cherry leaves after the spring fall of pink-white blossoms. Uninterested in the human pageant, it walked about beneath a red azalea bush, inspecting the raked earth for fat new grubs.

The American monk led us to the grave of Eisai, in a stone garden hidden behind old walls. Not far away was the grave of Myozen, where a very old man dressed in white sat on his heels among the mosses, paying the big gaijin no attention. "He was the head priest here," murmured our guide. "He's retired now, and spends his days pulling out the weeds in the stone gardens."

TO WHAT MAY THIS WORLD BE LIKENED?
MOONLIGHT IN A DEWDROP
FALLING FROM A DUCK'S BEAK.

EIHEI DOGEN

Harada–roshi (1871-1961)

At twenty, after thirteen years as a novice in the Soto school, Sogaku Harada had yet to meet an enlightened teacher. Dissatisfied, he entered a Rinzai monastery for seven years, then attended Komazawa Soto University in Tokyo, pursuing his Buddhist studies for some six years after graduation. Still unfulfilled, he continued to visit various Zen masters, asking about the great matter of life and death. At Engaku-ji, he was told by Soen Shaku, "If you experience kensho, your question will be answered all by itself." Resolved to pursue koan study, Harada went to Toyota Dokutan-roshi at Nanzen-ji, in Kyoto, one of the strongest Rinzai teachers of the day. Under Dokutan, his eye was opened, and eventually he received inka.

In 1921, when he was fifty, he accepted the post of abbot at Hosshin-ji, where he would teach for the next forty years. Before long, this small monastery on a dark and inhospitable coast won a reputation as the strictest in the country. Here the best of the Soto and Rinzai traditions has been merged in a fresh new manifestation of true Dharma. "Nobody has done real shikantaza since Dogen Zenji," Harada would declare, exhorting his students to ignore sectarian disputes and intensify rigorous zazen through koan study, which had all but disappeared from Soto Zen.

In an important sense, Harada-roshi was the first modern Zen master, and because he offered preparation for koan study – unheard of before this time – the more ferocious Zen students from all over Japan made winter pilgrimages to Hosshin-ji for the annual Rohatsu sesshin. The meditation hall, which seats perhaps thirty-five people, would overflow into the courtyard, all the way down to the small stream that crosses the lower court; at times there were several hundred monks doing zazen in the snow. Such conditions seemed ideal to the master, who approved of the wind and cold on this northern coast, the relentless rains off the Sea of Japan. Rude weather, he felt, lent itself nicely to introspection and the deep study of "the universe in the pit of one's own belly" that would eventually lead to letting the self go. Not surprisingly, a high percentage of his students attained a kensho.

"Harada talked a lot about listening," Tetsugen told me. "How when you go to teisho, you should be the only listener in the room. If there is just you and the teacher, you will listen: otherwise, you tend to give responsibility to others. And as you listen, doing zazen, there will no longer be two people in the room, no subject and object, just the One."

For Harada, as for Dogen and Hakuin, realization of the Buddha Way was not different from its actualization amid the tumult and temptations of everyday life.

If Harada-roshi never quit the priesthood, as he threatened, neither did he give up his battle with the Soto bureaucracy, which continued to obscure the purity of Dogen's teachings with petty sectarian disputes and rigid structuralism, setting up needless impediments to true Zen practice. Harada offended the Soto priesthood by placing so much emphasis on "Rinzai" koan study. At the same time, his views on formula responses that had made a mockery of koan study were very well-known. As one of his students, Soen Nakagawa, liked to say, "If the answers to koans are all that interest you, just bring a pad and pencil to the dokusan room and I will give them to you." Even after he became abbot of Ryutaku, Soen-roshi did not hesitate to put on his old monk's robe and travel across the main island of Japan to study with Harada-roshi, causing a great clicking of fans in the Rinzai hierarchy.

Soen first asked to study with Harada while still a hermit on Dai Bosatsu Mountain, near Mount Fuji, in the early thirties, but because Soto lacks Rinzai Zen's long, honorable tradition of "eccentrics," Harada had refused this bearded poet. Soen studied instead with Yamamoto Gempo-roshi at Ryutaku-ji, but even when he had completed his studies and received inka, he felt "incomplete." After Harada's death, Soen resumed study of the koan *Mu* with one of Harada's heirs, Hakuun Yasutani.

Although a Soto monk at age thirteen, Yasutani had spent years as a family man and schoolteacher, longing all this while for a true Zen master. Not until the age of forty did he find Harada-roshi, and at his first sesshin with Harada in 1925, he attained kensho with the koan *Mu*. Before meeting Harada, he recalled, "I was altogether a blind fellow, and my mind was not yet at rest. I was at a peak of mental anguish. When I felt I could not endure deceiving myself and others by untrue teaching and irresponsible sermons, my karma opened up and I was able to meet Sogaku Harada-roshi. The light of a lantern was brought to a dark night, to my profound joy."

At Hosshin-ji, some years later, Yasutani encountered Soen Nakagawa, who convinced him that Zen must travel to the West, and it was Yasutani who transmitted Harada's teachings to Soen and Eido, Yamada and Maezumi, Aitken and Tetsugen. In this way Sogaku Harada-roshi, whose nonsectarian teachings were carried to the New World by these Dharma heirs, became a great spiritual ancestor of American Zen.

Yasutani never returned to the United States; he died in March 1973, just prior to a planned journey to the United States for his ninetieth birthday. His friend Soen said:

Eighty-nine years, just-as-it-is!
How can I express, right now,
The grave importance of this very thing?

祖印大和尚壽像

129

Yamada-roshi (1907–1989)

In June of 1973, on the way to sesshin at Ryutaku-ji, Soen-roshi's students chanted and sat in zazen at the San-un zendo established here by Yasutani-roshi and administered by his disciple, Koun Yamada-roshi. Many years ago, at high school and at Imperial University in Tokyo, Yamada's roommate and close friend had been Soen Nakagawa. Inspired by Soen, Koun Yamada took up Zen studies under Yasutani-roshi and in 1953, following a stay at Ryutaku-ji, had a profound enlightenment experience.

Yamada-roshi had been absent on the day of that 1973 visit, but on this April Sunday, nine years later, a *zazen kai* – a day of sitting meditation – was just coming to an end when Tetsugen and I arrived in the late afternoon.

Although Yamada was ordained a monk and became Yasutani's first Dharma successor, he had no training as a priest and no longer shaves his head. At seventy-five, he is a big man of strong presence, with silvering dark hair, dark pouches like shadows beneath watchful eyes, and an expression of wry humor tinged with regret. "It is no exaggeration to say that Zen is on the verge of completely dying out here in Japan," Yamada has written. "Some people may think I am stretching the point, but sad to say, this is the actual state of affairs." Yasutani had also been of this opinion, and both teachers blamed it on the decline of zazen practice and of hard training directed toward "Attainment of the Emptiness of Mind."

Yamada told us that since returning from America in 1975, Soen-roshi has become a hermit; these days he saw nobody at all. Learning that I had once been Soen's student, he fetched a published volume of his old friend's haiku. "Soen-roshi is one of the great haiku poets, one of the very best in Japan. But he does not write haiku anymore. He is in pain from an old head injury. Also, he is suspicious of Western medicines, so he deals with the pain by taking too much sake." Yamada-roshi shrugged. We could visit Ryutaku-ji if we liked, but there was no hope that Soen-roshi would see us.

Soen Nakagawa-roshi (1907–1984)

I first met Soen-roshi on an August day in 1968, returning home to Sagaponack, Long Island, after a seven-month absence in Africa. I was astonished by the presence in my driveway of three inscrutable small men who turned out to be Japanese Zen masters. Hakuun Yasutani-roshi, eighty-four years old, was a light, gaunt figure with hollowed eyes and round, prominent ears; as I was to learn, he had spent much of the morning upside down, standing on his head in my driveway. Beside him, Nakagawa Soen-roshi, slit-eyed, elfin, and merry, entirely at ease and entirely aware at the same time, like a paused swallow, gave off emanations of lightly contained energy that made him seem much larger than he was. They were attended by Tai-san, now Shimano Eido-roshi.

Soen relates how once, in London, he was on the point of entering the bathroom when Christmas Humphreys, passing by, said it was occupied. The roshi waited there politely for a long time before he became concerned, after which he knocked, then opened the door. "Nobody there!" He laughed delightedly. "Wait as long as you like! Never anybody there! From the beginning!"

On his last visit to the United States, in 1975, Nakagawa Soen-roshi had scribbled on a scrap of paper his address at Ryutaku-ji. Whether I asked for it or whether he just gave it to me, I cannot recall. On another scrap he had scratched one of his haiku in quick Japanese characters:

In the light of flowers
I travel
Just for the sake of traveling.

Early in 1982, when I wrote to my old teacher that I would like to visit him in April, I received no answer. One of his disciples, Kyudo-roshi, assured me that his teacher would see no one. Sochu-roshi, Soen's successor as abbot of Ryutaku-ji, had informed Maezumi-roshi (who telephoned from Tokyo) that his old teacher was still in seclusion in his chamber high above the monastery, that he had let his hair grow long and had a beard, as in his hermit days on Dai Bosatsu Mountain, and that sometimes he was not seen for weeks at a time. This cloud-hidden state was confirmed by Soen's friend, Koun Yamada-roshi, at Kamakura. Yet my instinct was to pay my old teacher a visit "just for the sake of paying my old teacher a visit." If he would not see us, that was all right, too.

We will stay at Fuji Hannya Dojo, one of the lay meditation centers established by Joko-roshi, where Koryu-roshi still comes occasionally to give sesshin. Chido-sensei, who administers this dojo, is a small, sturdy man with beetling brows in a kind country face toughened by weather. Chido-sensei dresses simply in a black beret and dark blue sweat suit that seem to emphasize his isolation from the priesthood. With his daughter and pretty grandchildren, he lives among overgrown gardens of abounding roses, washed by restless winds in the tall evergreens, soothed by the rushing of the Kise River. The Kise flows down from the eastern slopes of Fuji-san, as this shining volcano, symbol of Eternal Mind, is known to the Japanese. Chido-sensei has known Soen for many years, and he and his friend Mr. Sakuma have many memories of that quixotic and beloved teacher, and laugh affectionately over old stories. "He hides himself now," Mr. Sakuma said, collecting himself with a polite sigh. "I have not seen him for some years."

At dawn our host led us in meditation in the small zendo, and afterward we carried flowers to Joko-roshi's grave on a wooded rise above the Kise River. His daughter served us a big country breakfast, and after breakfast Chido-sensei offered chanoyu. He served the ceremonial green tea precisely and correctly, yet simply, without mannerisms, the worn napkin small in his rough brown hand. His tea was "ordinary" in the sense so much admired by Zen masters, with nothing showy, "nothing special," nothing that drew attention to itself. ("Be more ordinary," Soen-roshi used to say to some of my more literary koan answers.) A fresh wind down off Fuji-san, high to the west, made a rushing sound in the great cryptomeria and strong bamboo, and the one sound strong enough to carry over wind and river was the light, sweet song of an unseen bird, lost in the leaves of a maple overhead.

Ryutaku-ji, the Dragon-Swamp Temple, is set on a steep slope of mosses and evergreens on the south side of the foothills of Mount Fuji. (The dragon symbolizes one's own true nature, or Buddha-nature, as in Dogen Senji's exhortation, "Do not be afraid of the true dragon!") At the entrance a monk said. "Soen-roshi is not so healthy now; he rises, falls. But he is feeling better today, and he will see you." Chidosensei translated these words, but because his English is haphazard, we wondered if the opposite message had been intended.

After making our bows in the main service hall where I sat sesshin in 1973, we went to the Founder's Hall to pay respects to Hakuin Ekaku, whose intensity animates an old wood statue that leans forward to peer into the eyes of those who look upon it. "His figure is extraordinary, he glares at people like a tiger, he walks like a bull; his power is fierce and difficult to approach," wrote Hakuin's disciple Torei Enji, who relocated the temple on this mountainside in 1761, the year that Hakuin came here to lecture. In the same place, two centuries later, at his shin-san-shiki, or abbot installation, Soen-roshi had worn Hakuin's robes.

Soen's successor, Sochu-roshi, had offered dokusan during the sesshin that preceded the formal opening of Dai Bosatsu, six years before, but our confrontations had been inconclusive. I remembered him best as one of the ringleaders on that lawless rowboat voyage to the Buddha on the farther side of Beecher Lake, and he had no reason to remember me at all. Though large, rounded, and thickset to the degree that Soen is small, erect, and trim, he resembles his teacher in his no-nonsense manner, his quick, cryptic humor, and his all but disreputable brown robes. Without bothering about greetings or introductions, he led us at once to an inspection of the new zendo, now under construction. The wood was still unstained and aromatic, and new copper tiles shined on the roof. At tea in the old monastery office, Sochu-roshi had little or nothing to say, and after a short time he rose rather abruptly and departed.

Quite suddenly, as if he had waited in the corridor for this moment, an old monk in a plain black robe stood in the doorway. He wore no sign of ordination, yet the robe was clean and his head was freshly shaven, and he stood erect in that authoritative way that had always made him seem larger than he was. Having expected an unkempt old man with long hair and beard, we were taken aback, and bowed in silence. Bowing briefly in return, Soen-roshi snapped, "All stand up, follow me." He turned on his heel and walked away toward the narrow stairs that led up the hillside to the abbot's rooms and eventually to his own small private chamber.

In 1973, the first morning of sesshin, Soen-roshi led his American students out of the service hall during dawn zazen, just as the first wand of light touched the old pond behind the monastery. At the foot of the stairs he pointed in silence at a dragonfly nymph that had crawled out of the lily pads and mud and fastened itself to the stair post. The nymph is a mud-colored water dweller of forbidding aspect and rapacious habit that preys on small fish and other creatures until the day comes when it hauls its heavy body from the water, affixes itself to wood or stone, and struggles to cast off its thick carapace, permitting its translucent, sun-filled dragonfly nature to take wing.

At sunrise, the new dragonfly was almost free, a beautiful golden thing, silvered by dew, resting a little, twitching its transparent wings, yet not quite liberated from the crude armor of its former life. When I gasped like the young monk on the mountain, unable to repress a delighted comment, Soen-roshi pointed sternly at the meditation hall: "Now do your best!"

Now it is 1982; in the reception room, Soen-roshi led us in the Kannon Sutra. Still very stern, the old teacher rose and we trailed him up the stair to the little chamber in the evergreens, overlooking the mossy hillside, the old fish pond, the old monastery. Once again I made my bows to the magnificent thousand-armed, thousand-eyed Kannon figure, a national treasure. Once again we chanted the Four Vows and the Gatha of Purification.

Only then did the roshi's stern expression soften in welcome. Greeting us one by one around the circle, he smiled, then laughed aloud in childlike pleasure. When my turn came, he took both of my hands and squeezed them three times, very hard, tears in his eyes, then rose to his knees and gave me a great hug. He laughed with Tetsugen, gazed at his old friend Chido-sensei with a happy smile. Then he went back around the circle, touching our heads in blessing, after which – just as he used to do – he commanded us to slap his shaved head hard, to knock some sense into it. By now, remembering his tricks, we were all laughing in delight.

Then, as if his eyes had died, he withdrew behind the remote expression I remembered so well from dokusan, in which his mouth sets as in a mask and his eyes disappear behind two slits. Without a word, he got up, bowed, and led us back down the crooked stair.

At the entrance he took up his long wood staff and marched along the woodland paths of Ryutaku-ji, leading the way down the mountainside to the public road where the cab would be waiting. On the forest path, he was still offering appreciation of his life, cheering a late-blooming cherry, pointing his long stave at the sun. "The sun, the moon are buddhas, all the human beings of this earth are buddhas, all is Buddha! Everything and everybody is a teacher. Sometimes you are my teachers, you are so-called roshi! Everybody is so-called roshi, okay? All is enlightened, as-it-is-now!"

All are nothing but flowers
In a flowering universe.

A little boy running uphill on the path, head down, was startled when he bumped into us, and more startled still when Soen-roshi, pointing his long stick, cried, "Monju! Here is Monju!" Monju is Manjusri, the Bodhisattva of Great Wisdom. The roshi was entreating us to perceive the Bodhisattva in the clear, undefended gaze of the little boy. Then the instant passed. Seeing the gaijin, the child's eye clouded in bewilderment, and the old man rubbed his head in blessing, saying sadly, "No, it is not Monju after all." The child ran off, and the roshi fell silent, walking on.

At the bottom of the hill where the cab was waiting, Soen-roshi was courtly and quiet. He inclined his head in recognition of our goodbyes, no longer with us, impatient to retreat into his solitude. Feeling incomplete, I told him how happy his students in America would be if he came to see them. I did not mention Eido-roshi and neither did he. "Perhaps," he said, "I shall appear soon in New York, but it is not a promise." He raised his staff and kept it raised as long as we could see him through the car window, a small, black-robed figure at the end of the path that led uphill into the forest.

Even before arriving in Japan, I had faith that Soen-roshi would see us, and this morning, as we drove up toward Mount Fuji, I felt sure of it. Tetsugen was mildly surprised that the visit had worked out so well in the face of so many obstacles and warnings. Tetsugen, too, perceives that Soen, with his ancient, innocent, and otherworldly ways, has the power of some old shaman from the Gobi Desert, and comes and goes, accountable to no one. Eido-roshi perceived him as "my greatest koan, truly ungraspable": Soen-roshi would say, "If I am caught, it is the end of me."

At seventy-five, Soen-roshi still seemed animated, but Tetsugen felt – and I had to agree – that he had been going on memory and nerve; his wild, spontaneous inspiration had dimmed. "He was almost like a ghost," Tetsugen commented as elation died in the journey down the mountain, "the perfect ghost of Soen-roshi, like a ghost in a Noh drama, which for some reason was allowed to reappear."

In the sadness attending our visit there was also freedom. The wonderful teachers who had brought the Dharma from Asia to the West would appear no more, but in another sense, they would be with us forever. In Western as in Eastern lands, the Buddha Way might need centuries to become established, so the sooner we got on about it, the better. It was time to step forward from the hundred-foot pole as the fortunate student of this American-born buddha who sits here beside me in this present, first, last, past, and future moment of my life.

"The Identity of Relative and Absolute"

The *Sandokai*, or "The Identity of Relative and Absolute", is a poem that was written by the Eighth Ancestor of Soto Zen, Sekito Kisen Zenji. It is part of the traditional liturgy of the Soto school and became such for its vivid and poetic description of the interplay and interpenetration of aspects of our lives. It is chanted daily in many Zen centers around the world. This English version was created in the early 1980s by Bernie Glassman and his student, Peter Matthiessen.

The mind of the Great Sage of India
Is intimately conveyed west and east.
Among human beings are wise ones and fools
In the Way there is no teacher of north and south.
The subtle Source is clear and bright;
The branching streams flow in the dark.
To be attached to things is primordial illusion;
To encounter the absolute is not yet enlightenment.
All spheres, every sense and field
intermingle even as they shine alone,
Interacting even as they merge,
Yet keeping their places in expressions of their own.
Forms differ primally in shape and character
And sounds in harsh or soothing tones.
The dark makes all words one;
The brightness distinguishes good and bad phrases.
The four elements return to their true nature
As a child to its mother.
Fire is hot, water is wet,
Wind moves and the earth is dense.
Eye and form, ear and sound, nose and smell,
Tongue and taste, the sweet and sour:
Each independent of the other
Like leaves that come from the same root.

And though leaves and root must go back to the Source
Both root and leaves have their own uses.
Light is also darkness,
But do not move with it as darkness.
Darkness is light;
Do not see it as light.
Light and darkness are not one, not two
Like the foot before and the foot behind in walking.
Each thing has its own being
Which is not different from its place and function.
The relative fits the absolute
As a box and its lid.
The absolute meets the relative
Like two arrow points that meet in midair.
Hearing this, simply perceive the Source,
Make no criterion.
If you do not see the Way,
You do not see it even as you walk on it.
When you walk the way you draw no nearer,
Progress no farther.
Who fails to see this
Is mountains and rivers away.
Listen, those who would pierce this subtle matter:
Do not waste your time by night or day!

Afterword

The face of American Zen has changed considerably in the twenty-five years since the writing of *Nine-Headed Dragon River*. There are more women practicing Zen, and many of them have become teachers and leaders of strong practice centers. There is a drift toward lay practice, in some form or another, along with a leveling out of the traditional hierarchy. There is an increasing amount of socially engaged activity in many sanghas. And the marketplace has provided for the emergence of different forms of commercial enterprise as a means of supporting practice communities.

Many of the Japanese teachers introduced in this book might have been surprised by these changes, but Maezumi-roshi was instrumental in encouraging or giving his students the leeway to open up the practice. We who practice now may take many of these changes for granted. We are accustomed to looking into the faces of our Dharma brothers and sisters, as we sit together in sesshin or in council. A recent trip to Japan with a group of Western Zen practitioners and teachers clearly revealed the differences between Zen in the West and in Japan. But all of those differences disappeared as we practiced together. I felt a deep connection to the teachers and places we visited, in particular with Yamamoto-roshi, Koryu-roshi's disciple with whom we sat at the Hannya Fuji Dojo, amidst birdsong, with the wind whispering in trees.

I feel so much gratitude to them and to all our ancestors for maintaining and passing on this simple, profound practice of freeing ourselves and all beings from attachment. Their examples remind us to renew our commitment to live our vows and embody our realization, and I remain grateful for the Dharma they passed on to us.

There is plenty of debate as to the pros and cons of the evolution of Zen, and whether or not we Americans are practicing an authentic form of Zen. This is an important question, and one which we should constantly ask ourselves, both as individuals and as organizations. In many ways, it seems to be true to the Mahayana ideal to practice profound inclusion, and yet we must be aware of the possibility of overdiluting the form that has been passed down to us over so many generations. So long as we remain committed to waking up and ending our suffering, so long as we remember that every step of the way is the way, so long as we see through and let go of our addiction to our selves, we'll all get home together.

Sensei Michel Engu Dobbs

CAPTIONS

The Descendants: Western Zen teachers, descendants in Maezumi-roshi's line, gather in Los Angeles in 2008. Each of these successors has developed his or her own style of teaching the Dharma; about half are females in a tradition that previously included exactly none. Zen Centers run by these teachers include those in New York, Massachusetts, Paris, New Jersey, San Diego, Salt Lake City, Ghent, Chicago, Tokyo, Oregon, Albuquerque, Germany, Poland, the Netherlands, Baltimore, Colorado, Los Angeles, Brazil, and Japan.

FIND YOUR OWN WAY.

TAIZAN MAEZUMI-ROSHI